STUDY GUIDE

Published by Arrows & Stones

Cover design by Sara Young
Cover photo by Andrew van Tilborgh

ISBN: 978-1-960678-99-7 1 2 3 4 5 6 7 8 9 10

Printed in the United States of America

unlocking the secret

lawrence powell

STUDY GUIDE

ARROWS & STONES

CONTENTS

unlocking the secret

the good life

lawrence powell

CHAPTER 1

THE ORIGINAL BLUEPRINT

You cannot dance with the devil and live the abundant life Jesus purchased for you.

READING TIME

As you read Chapter 1: "The Original Blueprint" in *The Good Life,* review, reflect on, and respond to the text by answering the following questions.

REFLECT AND TAKE ACTION:

What does the "abundant life" mean to you?

What does an abundant life look like?

What blueprint are you following? Who or what is the source of the original blueprint to abundant life?

> *Unless the LORD builds the house, they labor in vain who build it; unless the LORD guards the city, the watchman stays awake in vain.*
>
> **—Psalm 127:1**

Consider the scripture above and answer the following questions:

What stands out to you from this verse?

Have you let the Lord build your house? In what way?

What do you think may be holding you back from living the abundant life?

Do you believe the abundant life is available to you?

CHAPTER 2

THE GOSPEL OF GOOD SUCCESS

You don't have to be poor to be holy, and you don't have to be evil to be rich!

READING TIME

As you read Chapter 2: "The Gospel of Good Success" in *The Good Life*, review, reflect on, and respond to the text by answering the following questions

REVIEW, REFLECT, AND RESPOND

Does God desire for us to be successful? In what ways?

How can we come to know what God's will is?

When you recognize God's will, do you act accordingly? When have you done this in the past?

> *Beloved, I pray that you may prosper in all things and be in health, just as your soul prospers.*
>
> **—3 John 2**

Consider the scripture above and answer the following questions:

Do you believe God feels the same way about you as the writer of this verse did about his brother in Christ? Why or why not?

How can you apply the truth of this verse to your life?

What is God's top priority?

What all does God want to bless us with?

How can you "flip the switch" in your life and step into abundance?

What is the "Gospel of Good Success"?

CHAPTER 3

UNLOCKING THE SECRET

The power to make your way prosperous and secure success is found in the words which proceed out of your mouth.

READING TIME

As you read Chapter 3: "Unlocking the Secret" in *The Good Life*, review, reflect on, and respond to the text by answering the following questions.

REVIEW, REFLECT, AND RESPOND

How important is it to you to read God's Word?

How often are you in God's Word?

How do you study God's Word primarily? By yourself? In a small group? Through online resources?

This Book of Law shall not depart from your mouth, but you shall meditate in it day and night, that you may observe to do according to all that is written in it. For then you will make prosperous, and then you will have good success.

—Joshua 1:8

Consider the scripture above and answer the following questions:

What stands out to you from this verse?

____

____

____

____

____

____

What does it look like to meditate in God's Word day and night? Do you do this?

____

____

____

____

____

What kind of "good success" is this verse speaking of?

____

____

____

____

____

Do you ever catch yourself speaking negatively about yourself or your situation? How can you start speaking more positively?

____

____

____

____

____

____

What does the phrase "success does not happen by accident" mean?

____

____

____

____

____

How can you plan today for your success tomorrow?

____

____

____

____

____

What are some of your favorite promises from God's Word?

____

____

____

____

____

____

CHAPTER 4

SUCCESS: WHAT IT IS AND HOW TO OBTAIN IT

To be truly successful, you must fulfill the purpose for which you were created.

READING TIME

As you read Chapter 4: "Success: What It Is and How to Obtain It" in *The Good Life*, review, reflect on, and respond to the text by answering the following questions.

REVIEW, REFLECT, AND RESPOND

How would you define success personally?

How would the world define success?

What is success from God's perspective?

> *Wisdom is the principal thing; therefore get wisdom.*
> *And in all your getting, get understanding.*
>
> —Proverbs 4:7

Consider the scripture above and answer the following questions:

What does this scripture reveal about wisdom?

Where do we get wisdom from?

What's the difference between getting wisdom and getting understanding?

How are success and money tied together? What are their similarities, and where do they differ?

In what ways is success a goal?

How can you actually obtain success? What do you have to do?

What are the benefits of building your life upon the wisdom of God?

What is faith made up of?

What step can you take today to move you closer to your success?

CHAPTER 5

EIGHT ENEMIES OF SUCCESS

The successful person of tomorrow is the one who is not afraid of change today.

READING TIME

As you read Chapter 5: "Eight Enemies of Success" in *The Good Life*, review, reflect on, and respond to the text by answering the following questions.

REVIEW, REFLECT, AND RESPOND

Why and how is sin an enemy of success? How is the sin in your life holding you back from success?

____

____

____

____

____

____

Have you ever been guilty of having loose lips? How does having loose lips affect one's success?

____

____

____

____

____

____

When was the last time you broke a promise? Describe the situation. What was the result?

____

____

____

____

____

____

And whoever will not receive you nor hear your words, when you depart from that house or city, shake off the dust from your feet.

—Matthew 10:14

Consider the scripture above and answer the following questions:

What is the meaning of this verse?

How can you put this verse into action in your own life?

How can not forgiving others inhibit our success? Have you forgiven everyone you need to forgive?

What does "unfaithful stewardship" mean? Have you ever been guilty of this? Explain your answer.

What is "double-mindedness"? What is the danger of this?

Who do you spend the most time around? Are they positive influences in your life? Why or why not?

Are you willing to change to step into the abundant life that God has for you?

CHAPTER 6

HOW TO WIN AT WORK

Work not only releases your potential but it also activates your God-given energy and empowers you to produce.

READING TIME

As you read Chapter 6: "How to Win at Work" in *The Good Life,* review, reflect on, and respond to the text by answering the following questions.

REVIEW, REFLECT, AND RESPOND

Through what lens do you see your job? Are you blessed to have it? Is it a burden? Explain.

Is work required for success? In what way?

What four ingredients help us connect God to our work? Do you need more of any of these four ingredients?

> *Let your light so shine before men, that they may see your good works and glorify your Father in heaven.*
>
> **—Matthew 5:16**

Consider the scripture above and answer the following questions:

What is the meaning of this verse?

____

____

____

____

____

____

How can you practically apply this verse to your life?

____

____

____

____

____

____

What does it mean to live and work like a "real Christian"?

____

____

____

____

____

____

Do you feel your perspective towards your work could improve? Explain your answer.

Who's your true employer? Why is this important to remember?

Which of the bulleted principles listed at the end of this chapter do you need to work on? List all that may apply.

CHAPTER 7

THE TRUTH ABOUT MONEY

Money isn't something you only spend; it's a tool you can use.

READING TIME

As you read Chapter 7: "The Truth About Money" in *The Good Life*, review, reflect on, and respond to the text by answering the following questions.

REVIEW, REFLECT, AND RESPOND

Do you feel you have misconceptions about money?

Do you live as though God owns the money you make?

> *'The silver is Mine, and the gold is Mine,' says the LORD of hosts.*
>
> **—Haggai 2:8**

Consider the scripture above and answer the following questions:

What does this verse reveal about money?

____

____

____

____

____

How does this verse change your perspective about money, if at all?

____

____

____

____

____

Do you make your money, is it a gift from God, or is it 50-50? Explain.

____

____

____

____

____

____

____

____

What is the difference between wealth and money?

How can you use money as a tool?

What does the phrase "money talks" mean? Why is this important to understand?

Are there any money truths from this chapter that you were not aware of? How will they change your view and use of money now that you know them?

CHAPTER 8

MONEY MYTHS

Before there's a change in your checking account, there must be a change in between your temples.

READING TIME

As you read Chapter 8: "Money Myths" in *The Good Life*, review, reflect on, and respond to the text by answering the following questions.

REVIEW, REFLECT, AND RESPOND

Do you think money is inherently evil? Why or why not?

In what ways is money spiritual? How does your money reveal your heart?

> *For the love of money is a root of all kinds of evil, for which some have strayed from the faith in their greediness, and pierced themselves through with many sorrows.*
>
> —1 Timothy 6:10

Consider the scripture above and answer the following questions:

What is the "love of money" according to this verse?

How does this verse change your perspective of money, if at all?

Do you think money determines someone's happiness? Where does your happiness come from?

How can you make better decisions with money?

What would it look like if you showed more diligence with money?

Where can you exercise better discipline with money?

Did you previously fall for any of the money myths provided in this chapter? Which ones?

What financial habits or ways of thinking do you need to change most after reading this chapter?

GOOD

CHAPTER 9

TRUE RICHES

Do you trust your wealth, or do you trust in your God?

READING TIME

As you read Chapter 9: "True Riches" in *The Good Life*, review, reflect on, and respond to the text by answering the following questions.

REVIEW, REFLECT, AND RESPOND

In your own words, what are "true riches"?

> ***Wealth and riches will be in his house, and his righteousness endures forever.***
>
> **—Psalm 112:3**

Consider the scripture above and answer the following questions:

What stands out to you from this scripture?

What are the differences between "wealth" and "riches"?

Do you think money hinders someone from going to heaven? Why or why not?

Have you ever been guilty of trusting in your riches? Explain the situation and the outcome.

Are you missing any of the six elements of true biblical riches? If not, which do you most need to work on?

____

____

____

____

____

____

____

____

What are your priorities? Is God at the top of the list?

____

____

____

____

____

____

____

____

CHAPTER 10

THE MISSING LINK

If you want God to move on your behalf,
you need to move your behind!

READING TIME

As you read Chapter 10: "The Missing Link" in *The Good Life*, review, reflect on, and respond to the text by answering the following questions.

REVIEW, REFLECT, AND RESPOND

Do you have to put forth effort to live an abundant life? How much of it is in your control, and how much of it is a blessing from God?

Are you ready to take action? What in your life is holding you back?

Would you consider yourself to be diligent? How can you show more persistence?

> *"Now it shall come to pass, if you diligently obey the voice of the LORD your God, to observe carefully all His commandments which I command you today, that the LORD your God will set you high above all nations of earth."*
>
> **—Deuteronomy 28:1**

Consider the scripture above and answer the following questions:

What stands out to you from this verse?

____

____

____

____

____

What would it look like in your life if you "diligently obey the voice of the LORD"?

____

____

____

____

____

____

Which of the benefits of diligence provided in this chapter stand out to you? Are you reaping these four benefits in your life currently?

____

____

____

Are you ready to begin walking and living in everything that God has provided?

What is the first step you will take? How diligent will you be?

www.ingramcontent.com/pod-product-compliance
Lightning Source LLC
LaVergne TN
LVHW011053110826
845149LV00015B/3481

9781960678997